...dred islands in the chain, so this is not an exhaustive guide; the aim is to provide a few walks that represent the character of each of the main islands, while showcasing some of the many natural and historical attractions.

The islands are extremely diverse, and the walks described here, accordingly, extremely varied. The most northerly island – Lewis/Harris – is also the largest. On its eastern side is Stornoway: the largest town in the islands, with a population of around 8,000. The landscape of Lewis (*Walks 1-10*) is of wild moorland and peat; Harris (*11-18*) is more rocky and hilly, and includes An Cliseam (*Clisham*) (*12*), the highest peak in the islands.

Across the Sound of Harris are the linked islands of Berneray (*19,20,21*), North Uist (*22-25*), Benbecula (*26,27*), South Uist (*28-30*) and Eriskay (*31*). For the most part, these islands are low-lying (though there are hills on South Uist), with the land broken up by a multitude of salt and freshwater lochs. Beyond the Sound of Barra are the linked islands of Barra and Vatersay (*32-34*), islands so small and compact that the sea is rarely out of sight.

Very few generalisations about the landscape are possible, save that the western coasts tend to have wide beaches, battered by the Atlantic and the ever-present wind, while the eastern coasts are usually more rocky and sheltered.

The rocks of the Outer Hebrides are mostly Lewisian Gneiss: some of the oldest rock in the world, formed between 1,500 and 2,900 million years ago. This forms the backbone of the islands, occasionally jutting upwards to form rocky mountains, but mostly lying flat and covered with a layer of peat (perhaps up to 6 metres thick) or sandy earth (forming the machair grassland). This landscape gives the islands their atmosphere; the ancient rock emerging everywhere and giving a sense of both timelessness and stability. There are also several patches of granite in Harris. As elsewhere in Scotland, the landscape has been carved out by glaciation, leaving rough-hewn mountains and debris in low-lying areas.

The islands are littered with evidence of man's presence from the Neolithic period onwards. The ruins on many now deserted islands show how attractive the area's fishing and farming were in past times, as do the forts built on the islands to protect the inhabitants.

The earliest evidence of human habitation, from around 6,500 years ago, is in the form of chambered cairns used as burial monuments (24). Several important Neolithic sites exist on the islands, notably the standing stones at Callanish (7) (the second most important site in Britain after Stonehenge).

From 1000 BC to 500 AD, archaeological evidence (in the form of increased numbers of fortifications and weapons) suggest that the developing and expanding Pictish society was involved in warfare either internally or externally. From about 500 AD, the northward movement of the Irish 'Scotti' up the west coast undoubtedly changed the shape of the culture. Christianity was introduced, as shown by the number of early Christian sites on the islands.

14th-century church at Roghadal (Rodel)
(see Walk 18)

The Vikings came next, raiding, settling and conquering the whole of the Hebrides, both influencing and adapting to the local cultures. The Vikings were undoubtedly a major influence on the islands, and many of the place names are of Viking origin. Viking mills, homesteads and graveyards are dotted throughout the Hebrides.

Pieces from the famous Viking chess set found at Uig (Lewis)

The Western Isles remained under the control of the Vikings until 1266 when, following the Scottish victory at the Battle of Largs, the islands came under the rule of the Scottish crown. However, effective control was not established until 1598, when Stornoway became a burgh town. The intervening period was characterised by clan warfare and strife.

In 1745, at the start of the Jacobite rising, Bonnie Prince Charlie made his first landing on Scottish soil at the Prince's Beach on Eriskay (*31*). After the failure of the rising, in 1746, the fleeing Prince passed through Benbecula (*27*), Scalpay (*15*), Lewis and South Uist before crossing over the sea to Skye – the origin of *The Skye Boat Song* – on his way to the continent.

Reprisals for the uprisings and oppressive landlords marked the following century in most of the Highlands. Landowners increased their profits from the land by importing sheep and exporting residents. Ruined villages are testament to this process in the Hebrides, as are the large number of Scottish names taken to the New World by the emigrants.

The decimation of the islands' populations, due to both the Clearances and famine, was slowed somewhat by the introduction of the first Crofting Act in 1886. Although this legislation helped, land disputes continued into the next century. Vatersay (*34*) is famous for the Vatersay Raiders of 1907: a group of islanders who occupied the island, finally forcing a change in the legislation.

Reconstructed blackhouse village at Na Gearrannan, Lewis (see Walk 6)

In the 20th century the islands were strongly influenced by mainstream culture: the introduction of radio and television, the First and Second World Wars, the spread of the English language, modern transport and the lure of jobs on the mainland. Several industries emerged as mainstays of the islands' economies: fishing, crofting, weaving, and tourism. Other jobs came from the Merchant Navy and the Armed Forces.

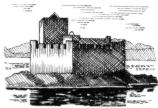

12th-century Kisimul Castle, which dominates Castlebay, Barra (see Walk 33)

The modern islands are a patchwork of the various influences they have experienced. Gaelic is still spoken by the majority of the islanders, although the dialect is heavily influenced by the centuries of Viking rule.

The islands' populations have stabilised, centred around traditional industries, tourism and pockets of high technology. The current rejuvenation of Gaelic culture has had a positive impact.

Religion remains a major influence on the islands; especially in Lewis and Harris, where the islanders strictly observe the Sabbath. While telecommunications and transport have made the islands more accessible, they are undoubtedly still a world apart from the mainland – not naïve or provincial, but less influenced by modern culture, and proud of their own traditions.

How to Get There

For transport purposes, the islands can be divided in three groups: **1)** Lewis/Harris and attached islands; **2)** the Uists, Benbecula and attached islands; and **3)** Barra and Vatersay. These three groups are linked by car ferries (*see* map). Island Hopscotch tickets are available.

1) Lewis can be reached by the Ullapool-Stornoway ferry, and also by air from Inverness, Glasgow and Edinburgh. Harris can be reached by the Uig (Isle of Skye)-Tarbert ferry.

2) North Uist can be reached by the Uig (Isle of Skye)-Lochmaddy ferry; South Uist by the Oban-Castlebay/Lochboisdale ferry; Benbecula by air from Glasgow.

3) Barra can be reached by the Oban-Castlebay/Lochboisdale ferry, and also by air from Glasgow.

All ferries are operated by Caledonian MacBrayne (08000 66 5000) *or* www.calmac.co.uk).

Gaelic in Place Names

In the Western Isles, many places have two names: one Gaelic and the other either English or an anglicised form of the original. Thus, 'Rubha Robhanais' is also 'Butt of Lewis' (*Walk 1*), and 'Calanais' is also the anglicised 'Callanish' (7). Both will usually appear on road signs. The newer Ordnance Survey maps use either both or only the Gaelic form.

In this guide, main island names have been left in their, more familiar, anglicised forms (eg, 'Lewis', 'Barra'). Main towns and ferry ports have been shown in their anglicised form first, with the Gaelic form in brackets after (eg 'Stornoway (*Steòrnabhagh*)'). Most other place names are shown only in their Gaelic form (eg 'Roghadal' rather than the anglicised 'Rodel'). (**NB:** those using older OS maps may have difficulty connecting some place names on their maps with those in this book).

Some common place name elements are listed and translated below (plus some of Norse origin). Please note that, since Gaelic is a heavily inflected language (ie, with changes to spelling depending on how a word is being used), some of these elements will not be instantly recognisable.

The link between Gaelic spelling and pronunciation is also confusing for beginners. For instance, the use of the aspirant 'h' after consonants – normally to indicate case or gender ('bàta'/'boat'; 'bhàta'/'of the boat') – leads to a change of pronunciation. An aspirated 'b' or 'm' gives a 'v' sound, so 'bhàta' is pronounced 'vata'.

A comparison of the Gaelic and anglicised place names in this book, and on road signs throughout the islands, will give some idea of the rules of Gaelic pronunciation. Good luck!

Common Place Name Elements

Abhainn – river
Acarsaid – anchorage
Allt – burn, stream
-aigh/-ay – island (Norse)
Baile – village/township
Bàgh – bay
Beag – small
Bealach – pass
Beinn – hill, mountain
-bost – farm (Norse)
Cairn – pile of stones, hill

Caol – narrow, strait
Clach – stone
Cnoc – hill
Creag/craig – rock, cliff
-dal/dail – valley (Norse)
Deas – south
Dubh – black
Dùn – fort
Ear – east
Eilean – island
Glas – grey
Iar – west
Lochan – small loch

Loidse – lodge
Machair – coastal grassland
Meall – hill
Mòr – big
-nis – headland (Norse)
Rubha – headland
Taobh – side
Tom – small hill
Tarbert – isthmus
Tràigh – beach
Tuath – north
-val – hill (Norse)

1 Eòropaidh Beach & the Butt of Lewis (*Rubha Robhanais*) —————————————

This splendid circular walk takes you along a quiet single-track road to the Butt of Lewis and its lighthouse, round the sea cliffs and back to a beautiful beach. Length: **4 miles/6.5km***; Height Climbed:* **90ft/30m***.*

From Stornoway (*Steòrnabhagh*), take the A857 to Barabhas then turn right towards Port Nis. Shortly before you reach Port Nis, turn left to Eòropaidh. There is a car park to the left of the road with a sign at the entrance for the Ness Coastal Path.

From here, walk back up to the road and turn left through the village. Look for the quiet single-track road signposted for Rubha Robhanais and follow it to the lighthouse. (It is worth making a diversion to see Teampall Mholuaidh (*St Moluag's Church*) before you leave the village.)

Just before the lighthouse, watch for a blue-topped waymarker post (coastal path) to your left. Turn off the road here and head for a second post, visible on the horizon. Beyond this, continue along the coast, quickly reaching a deep, rocky inlet (take care). A gate takes you through a fence at the head of the inlet, beyond which you follow a line of well-spaced posts along the coast.

At the top of the small beach at Cunndal there is another gate. Go through this then edge left to cross a small stream above a gully.

Go past the beach, round a field covered with lazy-beds and through a gate close to the sea. Follow the coast round to another gate and then back

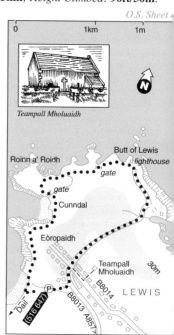

O.S. Sheet

Teampall Mholuaidh

Roinn a' Roidh

Butt of Lewis lighthouse

gate

gate

Cunndal

Eòropaidh

Teampall Mholuaidh

30m

B8014

B8013 A857

LEWIS

Dail

516 647

down to the beach at Eòropaidh.

If you wish to walk further along the coast, the blue-topped posts continue from the southern end of the beach, through machair and fine coastal scenery, as far as the beach below Dail: an additional distance of 2 miles/3km.

tough, linear coastal walk. There is no path in places and you will eed good waterproof footwear. The route follows the coast, through oorland and past small lochs. There are various historic sites on e way and a fine view of Lewis's eastern sea cliffs. Length: up to **10 iles/16km** *(one way); Height Climbed: undulating. This route can be alked either way, but is described from the south.*

O.S. Sheet 8

rive about 10 miles north from ornoway (*Steòrnabhagh*) on the 895 – marked Tolsta (*Tolastadh*) until the road ends at the car park Tràigh Ghearadha. The walk starts rom the car park (where there is an nformation board) and is signposted.

A paved single-track road runs to e 'Bridge to Nowhere' (part of a oad started by Lord Leverhulme, but ever completed) and soon becomes a vide grassy track along the coast.

Follow the yellow waymarkers long the track and then over the oggy moor. There is no real path, ut from each marker you should be ble to see the next one even when it s quite far away. The path zig-zags ently between the coast and the land, assing close by numerous lochs.

The journey is punctuated by istoric sites, such as the solitary ouse of a soldier from the 820's whose entire family were ispossessed, the ruin of a chapel, eserted houses perched on the sea liff, and a memorial to a young man vho fell into the ocean while trying to ollect birds' eggs from the cliffs.

The track widens to an unsurfaced oad near the end of the walk, efore finishing at the village of

Sgiogarstaigh, near the north end of Lewis.

3 Barabhas & Brù

This walk passes three small lochs and links two villages on tracks and rough paths. Although the route is waymarked, the path disappears in places and navigation may be required. Length: 5½ miles/9km; Height Climbed: 120ft/40m.

O.S. Sheet 8

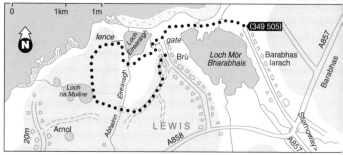

From Stornoway (Steòrnabhagh), follow the A857 to the junction with the A858. Continue on the A857 for a short distance then turn first left onto a minor road (Sraid na Loch). Follow this road to the end of Barabhas Iarach. Park here then follow a rough track to a bridge over a burn then on round the bottom of Loch Mòr Bharabhais. Cross a second bridge, over the outflow from the loch, then continue to join a metalled track below the village of Brù.

Go up the road towards a gate and, just before it, turn right along a fence. When a second fence crosses the way turn left through/over a gate and continue in the original direction on a peat track along the top of Loch Èirearaigh. The route then crosses a bridge and continues around the loch.

You reach a fence with a gate in it. Do not go through the gate: climb to your left to reach a post, then follow the line of posts beyond, over a hill and down to cross a gully. Aim left beyond this to reach a stile at a junction of fences. Cross the stile and walk on with a fence to your right to reach Loch na Muilne.

You reach a waymarker at the end of the loch and turn to the left. From this point the waymarkers can be difficult to follow. You cross some rough, boggy ground to reach a good bridge over Abhainn Èirearaigh. After crossing the bridge, follow the waymarkers to join a clear peat track. Almost immediately this joins another track. Go left, heading back to the village. The track splits just before you reach the village. Take the left-hand path, then go left again through Brù to return to the bottom of the village.

Retrace your steps to the start.

4 Abhainn Ghriais _____ B

This lineal walk follows a vehicle track up a moorland glen. It gives a good flavour of the peaty interior of Lewis, and there are views of the coast on the return route. Length: 6¹/₂ miles/10.4km (there and back); Height Climbed: 180ft/60m. It is possible to combine this walk with a visit to Tràigh Ghriais – a fine sandy beach.

O.S. Sheet 8

From the centre of Stornoway (*Steòrnabhagh*), head north on the A857, then turn right onto the road to Tolastadh (B895). After about 8 miles the road crosses a bridge and passes a cemetery. There is a car park and picnic site to the right of the road just beyond this.

From the car park, cross the road (carefully) and walk up the minor road opposite, signposted to Griais village. Walk up through scattered housing. At the top of the road you reach a four-way junction by a post box. Go left here, on a metalled road. Go through a gate and follow the path beyond down to a footbridge over the Abhainn Ghriais.

Cross the river, climb to a metalled road and turn right. This road ends at a skip site, just beyond, and you continue along a clear track. Continue climbing on this track, through new woodland planting at first, with the river off to your right, ignoring several junctions.

The track eventually returns to the river and doubles back for a short distance. When it ends, continue along the bank for a short distance on a sheep path to reach a small ruined hut – worth a look before you return.

Return by the same route. A

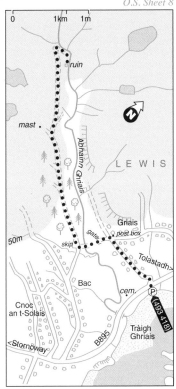

footpath from the car park leads down to the fine sandy beach at Tràigh Ghriais.

5 Lews Castle Grounds _____ C

*A terrific parkland and coastal walk in the grounds of Lews Castle, right in the centre of Stornoway (Steòrnabhagh). The landscaped grounds, with their fine woodlands, also provide a number of additional paths to explore. Length: **4 miles/6.4km**; Height Climbed: **165ft/50m**.*

O.S. Sheet 8

Lews Castle was built in the 1840s by a former owner of Lewis, James Matheson. He surrounded his home with an area of splendid mixed woodland. The castle grounds were gifted to the town in 1924 by Lord Leverhulme, and much work has been undertaken to restore the fine collection of plants and trees.

To reach the start of the walk, follow Cromwell Street from the Tourist Information Centre. Continue, as it becomes Bayhead, until you see the distinctive castle gates on your left. Once inside the castle grounds turn left at the sign for the Woodland Centre and Cuddy Point.

The path quickly joins the river and follows it downstream, as it widens into Stornoway Harbour. Follow the path past the Woodland Centre (which has an excellent café/bar) and continue along the clear track by the wooded shore.

The path eventually reaches a small bay with a wooded island in it and turns right, up the River Creed. Follow the track to a junction by a footbridge and turn right.

The track crosses the higher ground. Keep left at the first junction and right at the second to re-enter the parkland. Follow the track past the monument to James Matheson and Lews Castle to return to the start.

Lews Castle

6 Coastal Walk _____ A/B

A long waymarked walk following old paths between villages on the beautiful north-west coast of Lewis. The walk is rarely far from a village, so it can be broken up if desired. Length: **10¹/₂ miles/17km** *(one way); Height Climbed:* **240ft/80m** *(undulating).*

O.S. Sheet 8

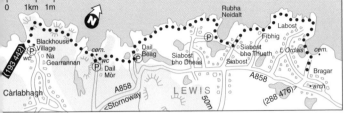

From Stornoway (*Steòrnabhagh*), follow the A859 for 6 miles to Luirbost and turn right to join the A858. Follow this to Càrlabhagh and take the minor road to Na Gearrannan, following the signs to the Blackhouse Village. Drive down to the village, where there is a car park.

Walk through the village to a signboard showing the route, and the start of the waymarkers. Go through a gate and along a grassy path up the hillside. The markers largely follow the coastline.

The path leads through a more hilly section, across a stream (on some stepping-stones), and then round a steep hillside. A zig-zag descent takes you past a graveyard to the quiet beach at Dail Mòr, where the waymarkers disappear.

The path reappears a little way up the road, on your left, and leads over a hill to Dail Beag. Follow the waymarkers and the path ultimately joins the public road. Turn left and follow the road down to the sea.

At the end of the road, there is an information board and the path continues. Don't take the obvious path round to the sea cliffs, but follow the waymarkers straight up and over a stile. Further on there is a stone wall, which you need to climb.

The path then follows the coast. Take care going past the bottom of Siabost bho Dheas; there is an open hole with the sea below. Continue round Rubha Neidalt, then round the shore, across a causeway and into Siabost bho Thuath. When you reach a T-junction in the village turn left and follow the road down to a gate.

From this point, the walk is flatter, running round the coast past Fìbhig and Labost (there is no clear path: watch for a series of posts and red stiles), between Loch Ordais and the sea, to an information point at the bottom of Bragar. From here, follow the road up to the village – note the whalebone arch.

*The impressive standing stones at Callanish are one of the most
important archaeological sites in Britain. This walk takes you from the
visitor centre round to the two satellite circles, then back to the main
site. Length:* **2 miles/3.5km***; Height Climbed: none.*

O.S. Sheet 8

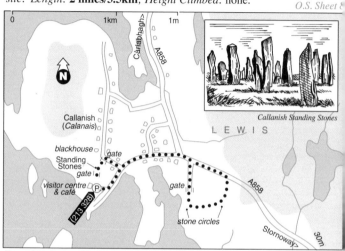

Callanish Standing Stones

From Stornoway (*Steòrnabhagh*),
follow the A859 for 6 miles to
Luirbost and turn right to join the
A858. Follow this for 8 miles then
turn left at the sign for the visitor
centre. From the parking place
outside the visitor centre, walk back
along the quiet road to the A858.
Turn right along the main road for
about 200m then turn right again onto
a single-track road. This leads down
to a gate, and beyond that to the first
satellite circle. Look over to the hill
above the visitor centre for views of
the main site. Take a muddy path to
the second satellite circle and then

back to the road at a lay-by.

From the lay-by, walk back
towards the visitor centre but, shortly
before you reach it, turn right up
a small steep road marked 'No Ice
Gritting Beyond This Point' and '15%
unsuitable for coaches'. Take this
lane up a short steep hill, and through
a gate on your left, which takes you
to the main Standing Stones. Please
stay on the perimeter path to avoid
damaging the site. To return to the
visitor centre and the parking place,
go through a gate at the other end
of the enclosure and along a well-
surfaced path.

This pleasant walk up the west side of Great Bernera (Beàrnaraigh) leads to an iron-age village at Bostadh. Length: 2¹/₂ miles/4km (one way; 6¹/₂ miles/10.5km if return by road); Height Climbed: 180ft/60m.

O.S. Sheet 13

Iron-Age House

Follow the A859 from Stornoway (Steòrnabhagh) for 6 miles to Luirbost, then turn right to join the A858. Follow this for 5 miles and turn left onto the B8011. After 3 miles, turn right onto the B8059 to Bernera.

Follow the road across the bridge and on to Breacleit. Park at the Community Centre (tea room) and walk on along the road to Bhalasaigh. The road ends at a turning place. Turn left over a footbridge and follow a concrete path to the right of a house. As you approach a second house go right, through a gate, and aim for a post visible on a small hill.

Beyond this, go through a gate in a fence then follow the blue-topped waymarker posts along the coast until you reach a post with a blue arrow on it, pointing right. This leads you across a marshy section between the coast and a small inland loch. Continue along the path (ignoring a gate in a fence to your right) to reach the public road at Tobson.

Turn left along the road, then left again at the junction. Just past a building there is a gate on the right.

Go through the gate and walk straight up the grassy slope ahead, following posts to reach a cairn/post at the top of the hill. Ahead you will see another cairn, on the top of a hill. Aim for this but go through a gate in a fence at the low point then turn right, with Loch a' Sgail to your right.

Follow the path through two gates then edge left down a grassy valley. At the bottom of the valley you will see a reconstructed iron-age house above a small beach. Turn right (across a footbridge) above this house and follow the right-hand edge of the cemetery to reach the road.

Return the same way, or take the road back to Breacleit.

9 The Beehive Dwellings ———————————— B

These unusually-shaped dwellings are well worth the boggy walk from the road. Length: **5 miles/8km** *(there and back); Height Climbed:* **180ft/60m**. *For experienced walkers, the walk could be extended by continuing up the glen, or by an ascent of Scalabhal on the way back (map and compass needed).* **Grazing cattle: take care.**

O.S. Sheet 13

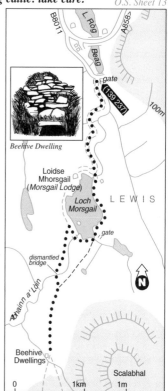

Beehive Dwelling

Follow the A859 from Stornoway (*Steòrnabhagh*) for 6 miles to Luirbost, then turn right to join the A858. Follow this for 5 miles and turn left onto the B8011. Follow this for 8 miles until it crosses the head of Loch Ròg Beag, then turn second left onto a single-track road marked 'Kinloch Roag'. Follow this to the gate at the end of the road to Morsgail Lodge. Park somewhere here, being careful not to cause obstruction.

Go through the gate and follow the road up towards the lodge. Just before you reach Loch Morsgail, turn left over a small bridge. At the far end turn right, by the side of the loch.

Near the south end of the loch you cross a small burn (you pass close by a rusted gate just before the crossing). Continue along the side of the loch to reach a bridge over Abhainn a' Lòin (**NB:** if the burns are in spate you should head left at this point and rejoin the route on the old track south of Abhainn a' Lòin – *see map*).

Walk on beyond the bridge until, roughly level with the island in the loch, a faint path heads back-left. Follow this to the point where a bridge once crossed Abhainn a' Lòin. Ford the burn here and follow a muddy track beyond. You will find the beehive dwellings on the near side of the first major tributary you reach.

Return by the same route.

This landrover track leads from near Timsgearraidh over a bealach (pass) and down to Loch Cheann Chuisil, giving a hill walking experience without leaving a good track. The track is an access road to a house by the loch, so please respect the owner's privacy. Length: up to **12¹/₂ miles/20km** (there and back)*; Height Climbed:* **825ft/275m**.

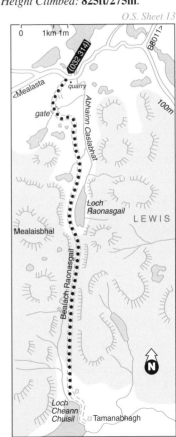

O.S. Sheet 13

Follow the A859 from Stornoway (*Steòrnabhagh*) for 6 miles to Luirbost, then turn right to join the A858. Follow this for 5 miles and turn left onto the B8011. Follow this for 17 miles until a road cuts right for Timsgearraidh then carry on for a further 3 miles on the minor road leading round to the south side of the sandy beach of Tràigh Uige (if you wish to visit the beach, a right turn after 2 miles leads to a car park).

Cross a small bridge then turn left following signs for Mangersta. After a short distance you pass the entrance to a quarry to your left, with the end of a vehicle track just beyond it. Park somewhere near here (avoiding obstructing entrances) and start walking down the track.

After a short distance the track splits. Follow the main (right-hand) track, straight ahead. This leads down to a gate. Walk round this and continue up to Loch Raonasgail.

The track leads up and over the bealach, with impressive views of the mountains on either side, then descends gently to the sea at Loch Cheann Chuisil.

The side of the loch is a pleasant place for a rest before returning by the same route.

This walk crosses a high hill pass and passes four inland lochs. Towards the end it runs along the top of some sea cliffs. Length: up to **7 miles/ 11km** *(one way: 12 miles/19km, in total, if you return by the public road); Height Climbed:* **630ft/210m**. *For a shorter alternative, the scenic path from Huisinis to Crabhadail is worth exploring.*

O.S. Sheet 13

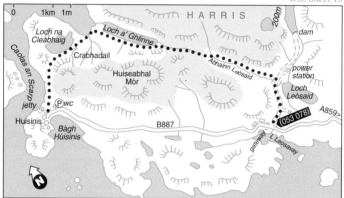

From Tarbert (*An Tairbeart*), take the A859 north for three miles then turn left onto the B887 for Huisinis. Follow this for about 7½ miles to the point where a single-track road heads off to the right to a power station. Park near the end of the power station road and start walking up it.

Follow it for a little under a mile/ 1.5km until you come to a bridge crossing the Abhainn Leòsaid. Cross this, turn left off the track, and follow a faint path by the burn as it climbs through Gleann Leòsaid. After 2 miles/3km of gentle ascent, the path descends more steeply to Loch a' Ghlinne.

When you reach the loch, head left to walk down its south side. This is rough walking. At the end of the loch keep straight on to reach the sandy beach. Turn left, along the beach, then cross a low hill to reach the white cottage by Loch na Cleabhaig.

From the cottage, follow the faint path along the side of the loch. When the loch shore bends away keep straight on, climbing to a hill pass. Beyond this the path runs across a steep, dramatic slope before leading down, through two gates, to the jetty overlooking Caolas an Scarp. Follow a track across the narrow neck of land to reach the village of Huisinis.

Return by the same route or along the road (a shorter alternative).

*An Cliseam (799m) is the highest hill in the Western Isles, and gives
outstanding views over the surrounding landscape. It is a tough walk
– only for the experienced – but well worth the effort. Length:*
6 miles/10km (there and back)*; Height Climbed:* **2150ft/650m**.

O.S. Sheet 13 or 14

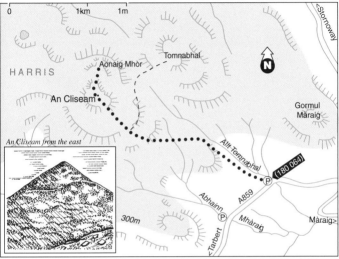

An Cliseam from the east

From Tarbert (*An Tairbeart*), follow
the A859 north and park in the
second car park before the turn off to
Màraig and Reinigeadal, next to Allt
Tomnabhal (Grid Ref 180 064). Walk
up the left-hand side of the river until
the glen loses its steep sides. At this
point head left, towards An Cliseam.
Head for the eastern slope and ascend
the obvious ridge.

A path starts to form as the ridge
narrows and becomes rocky. Near
the summit, there are large drops
on either side and boulders make

the walking difficult. The path is
intermittent, but follow the ridge
along to the trig point, and then along
to the rocky outcrop of Aonaig Mhòr
for views to the north.

Experienced hillwalkers will find
their way to neighbouring peaks. For
this route, descend by the same route.
If you want to walk round Tomnabhal
and Gormul Màraig, contour round
An Cliseam at about 550m, keeping
as much altitude as possible, and
crossing the tributaries of Allt
Tomnabhal.

A low-level walk along the line of an old road that gives the impression of being much further from civilisation than it is. There are good views of the hills and lochs. Length: **4 miles/6km** *(one way); Height Climbed:* **400ft/135m**. *You can start this walk from Urgha near Tarbert (An Tairbeart) by following the directions for Walk 14 but stopping at a lay-by on top of a hill before you reach Loch Lacasdail. From there the walk is signposted. Here, it is described the other way, so that you have the opportunity of making a circular route with Walk 14.*

Drive north from Tarbert (*An Tairbeart*) on the A859 towards Stornoway (*Steòrnabhagh*) for 8 miles, then turn right onto the road signposted to Reinigeadal and Màraig. Drop down to a hairpin bend and look for a sign for the path to Urgha. There is limited parking on the verge near here.

Start walking along the clear path – part of the Frith-Rathad na Hearadh (*The Harris Walkway*). The path drops to cross two bridges then climbs to join a path coming in from the left. Turn right along this. This was originally the old road leading north from Tarbert. (The old road provides an alternative start to this walk, and can be used to complete the loop with Walk 14 – *see* map.)

The path climbs to a cairn in a low pass – from where there are great views down Loch Lacasdail and beyond across Loch an Tairbeairt – then descends, contouring round to the right. It then runs along the side of scenic Loch Lacasdail.

Stay on the near side of the loch and the path soon climbs to join the road at a lay-by. Here there is

O.S. Sheet 14

an interpretative panel with a map showing this route and the possible loop using Walk 14 (making a circuit with a total length of 11$\frac{1}{2}$ miles/18km). If you wish to complete the circuit, turn left along the road; otherwise, return by the same route.

14 Urgha to Reinigeadal _____ A

The road leading to the village of Reinigeadal was only completed in 1989, and the villagers and schoolchildren regularly used this path until then. It is now a fairly quiet footpath, offering excellent views and passing through a deserted village. Length: 3½ miles/5.5km (one way); Height Climbed: 1200ft/370m. Possible link with Walk 13.

O.S. Sheet 14

From Tarbert (*An Tairbeart*), take the Urgha/Scalpay road east for about two miles. Just after crossing the bridge at the bottom of Loch Lacasdail you will see a small lay-by on your left where you can park. The path is signposted.

Follow a muddy but well-defined path, heading up into the hills. The path continues, climbing steadily to a pass between Beinn Tharsuinn to the south and Trolamul. There is a cairn at the highest point of the pass.

A short distance down the other side an indistinct path leads off to the right (this leads to the abandoned village of Molingeanais). For this route, continue on the main path as it curves downwards to the left, then turns into a steep and slippery descent down to Loch Trolamaraig.

Cross a bridge at the head of the loch. Just beyond this the path splits. The left-hand path, climbing past an impressive boulder, is less eroded. The paths quickly join up again.

The path climbs over a headland before another grassy descent takes you back down to the coastline. Go through a small gate and make your way through some deserted but picturesque blackhouses. Beyond these the now muddy path climbs up through another gate and onto the road. Turn right to reach the little village of Reinigeadal.

Either return by the same route or, to join up with Walk 13, walk from Reinigeadal back along the quiet single-track road for approximately 4 miles. The total length of this circuit is 11½ miles/18km.

Walks Western Isles

Grades

A+
Full walking equipment
– including map and compass
– and previous hill walking
experience essential

A
Full walking equipment
required

B
Strong walking footwear and
waterproof clothing required

C
Comfortable walking foot-
wear recommended

B/C, etc
Split grades refer either to
multiple route titles or to the
fact that the single route described can be walked either
in its entirety or in shorter,
less gruelling sections.

NB: Assume each walk increases at
least one grade in winter conditions.
Hill routes can become treacherous.

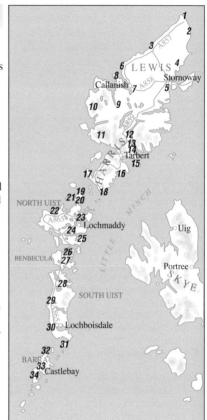

Published by: Hallewell Publications, The Milton, Foss,
Pitlochry, Perthshire PH16 5NQ
Printed by: J. Thomson Printers, Glasgow

Walks Western Isles

Scalpay (Scalpaigh) is a small island, connected to Harris by a handsome bridge. Eilean Glas Lighthouse (1789), on the eastern edge of the island, provides a spectacular viewpoint across The Minch to Skye. Length: **3 miles/5km** *(there and back); Height Climbed:* **135ft/ 45m**. *Route waymarked, but rough and boggy in places.*

O.S. Sheet 14

From Tarbert (*An Tairbeart*), follow signs for Scalpay. Once across the bridge you quickly reach a T-junction. Go left (Ceann a Bhaigh). Follow this road past the school in the village and keep straight on at the junction just beyond. Follow the road out of the village and along the coast. Keep straight on at a further junction and continue to the turning area at the end of the road. Do not park in this turning area; park by the road further back (avoiding obstructing entrances).

The walk begins about 80m back up the road from the turning place, at the first waymarker. Head up a small hill onto a muddy track. This soon disappears into the bog, but the first waymarkers are easy to follow.

Go over the headland, cross a stile over a fence, and descend the grassy slope below. Several muddy paths cut

off to the right between waymarkers 6,7 and 8, but don't follow them. The route leads downhill and straight ahead, through a rocky gully, to waymarker 8.

The path climbs up a small rise, to waymarker 10, then down the grassy slope towards the sea. Waymarker 11 is at the bottom of the slope. The path continues round the coast, with the waymarkers appearing on the horizon and the lighthouse often visible in the distance. There are a few small gullies to be crossed, so take care.

Past waymarker 18, walk on a short distance to reach the wall around the lighthouse grounds. Turn left along the wall until you come to a gate. Go through this and descend until you reach a stone path. Follow this to the deserted lighthouse.

Return the same way.

16 **Bealach Eòrabhat** _____ **B**

This bealach (pass) joins the contrasting east and west coasts of South Harris, following an old coffin route. Boggy in places. Length: 3½ **miles/5.6km** *(one way); Height Climbed:* **310ft/103m** *(on return route). Return by the old road makes a total of 8 miles/14km.*

O.S. Sheet 14

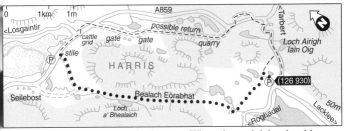

From Tarbert (*An Tairbeart*), take the road south for four miles, then turn left on the road signposted Roghadal. Follow this for a mile until the road to Lacklee cuts off to the left. At this point there is a small car park to the right of the road.

Take the signposted track just before the car park. This leads to a sheep fank. Pass to the left of this and continue for a short distance to reach a T-junction with another path. Turn left along this (sign).

The path joins a fence, crosses a low hill then zig-zags down to a footbridge over a burn with a house beyond. Cross the bridge and turn right, between the burn and a garage, to see the next post. The path now leads gently up to the bealach.

The top of the pass is broad and peaty, and gives fantastic views down to the west coast. The track descends gently, broadening as it runs along the side of Loch a' Bhealaich.

Where the track joins the old road there is a sign and the option of going left to Seilebost, back over the bealach or following the old road back to the car. To do the latter, go right and follow the old road, passing through several gates, until it joins the main A859 at a stile.

Go right on the main road and follow it past the turn off to Losgaintir. Just beyond a cattle grid, take the old road which starts to the left. Follow this until it rejoins the main road. Follow this for 250m then turn right – at the sign for Laxadale Cottage – back onto the old road. Follow the road past the cottage and a small loch, then over a hill to a quarry (blasting: obey notices).

Continue back up to the main road. Cross this and rejoin the old road – first above and then below the main road – following it until it joins the Roghadal road by a sub station. Turn right to reach the start.

A beautiful walk across the machair followed by a stiff hill climb, offering fine views across the Sound of Taransay. The path to the ruined chapel provides a pleasant extension (or shorter walk). **Length: 5 miles/ 8km** (there and back)*; Height Climbed:* **1095ft/365m**.

O.S. Sheet 18

Drive to the village of Taobh Tuath, off the main road (A859) between Tarbert (*An Tairbeart*) and Roghadal (five miles north of the latter). Follow the road through Taobh Tuath and park at the unmanned MacGillivray Centre, to the right at the end of the village. Walk on along the road, and keep straight on at a junction to reach a gate at the end of the road.

Go through the gate, walk along a sandy track, then through another gate, to where the path splits in four. An arrow shows the correct route: ahead and slightly to the left. Follow this sandy path as it leads to the end of the beach, and then becomes a grassy track running along the coast. Follow this to a third gate, where you have a choice.

To reach the ruined chapel from here go through the gate. The 16th-century chapel on Rubh' an Teampaill is visible ahead. **To climb Ceapabhal**, don't go through the gate, but look uphill to see a small gate in a fence on the other side of a stone wall.

Go through this gate, and climb up onto the shoulder of the hill beyond. From here, make your way up the main ridge. Although there is no path the route is fairly obvious, though extremely hard work.

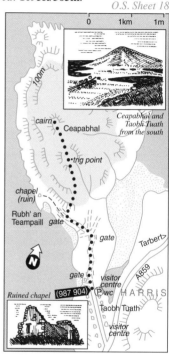

Ceapabhal and Taobh Tuath from the south

The steep climb finally levels out and a peaty path leads across the high moorland to the trig point. There are fantastic views both from here and from the cairn further down the ridge. Descend by the same route, taking care on the steep grassy, rocky slopes.

18 Roghadal to Renish Point (*Rubha Reinis*)_____ B

The first part of this walk, to Borrisdale (Borghasdal), is on a good path, but there is no path from here to Renish Point, and the ground can be boggy. The walker is rewarded with good views. Roghadal is notable for St Clement's: a restored medieval church. Length: **5 miles/8km** *(there and back); Height Climbed:* undulating.

O.S. Sheet 18

From Roghadal, go back down the A859 from St Clement's Church for about 200m and look for a track starting to the left, signposted to Borrisdale. Follow the track across a small bridge then turn off it onto a grassy path. This path splits almost immediately (post). Take the left-hand path (ie, go straight on) and climb the hillside ahead.

Follow this until you reach a fence, which you should follow up to the right. This leads you along the top of some small cliffs to a gate. Go through this and follow the path beyond along the loch, over a small bridge, uphill to another gate, then up through a field to join the driveway to a house. Turn left along this to reach the road, then turn right.

Follow the road as it runs gently downhill, then take the first left. This will lead you to a turning place at the end of the road. Go through a gate on the right and walk up to a sheep fank, then go through another gate. After another fence and another gate go left, along the fence, to join a sheep track which runs along the east side of the headland.

Follow this until you reach an old fence across the headland. Turn right along the fence to reach a small gate.

Go through the gate and stay on the higher ground on your left to avoid the bogs. From the end of the strip of high ground you can see a cairn on the horizon, between two small hills.

Aim for the cairn, choosing the best route to avoid the bogs. Once you reach the gully between two small hills, take the easiest way up to the cairn. From here you get a good view down to the headland and you can easily walk down to the point.

Return by the same route.

19 Beinn a' Chlaidh / 20 Beinn Shleibhe ————— C/B

Two climbs to viewpoints on the island of Berneray (Beàrnaraigh).
19) *A short ascent to a standing stone and a low summit with fine views.*
Length: **1 mile/1.5km**; *Height Climbed:* **100ft/30m**. **20)** *An easy climb to a spectacular viewpoint.* *Length:* **2 miles/3.2km** (there and back); *Height Climbed:* **300ft/90m**.

O.S. Sheet 18

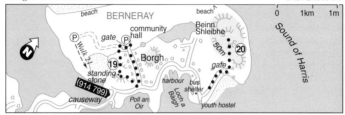

To reach Berneray, take the A865 north from Lochmaddy (*Loch nam Madadh*). After 5 miles turn right at the sign and cross the causeway.

Walk 19) After crossing the causeway keep right at a junction (Borgh) then left at the next (Borgh). Continue to the end of the road and park in the car park at the hall.

Leave the car park and turn right through a gate onto a tarred track (this leads to a further car park which gives access to the beach). Beinn a' Chlaidh is the low hill on your left. You can see a waymarker post on the skyline. Head straight for this and then follow the posts to the standing stone and the low summit.

Looking back-left from the summit you will see another post. Follow the faint path to this post, then continue towards the coast. Further posts will lead you down to the road by the head of Poll an Oir. Follow the road back to the start of the walk.

Walk 20) Follow the driving instructions as for Walk 19, but do not take the second turn into Borgh; instead, follow the coast road past the harbour and round Loch a Bhàigh until you reach a junction by a bus shelter. Turn sharp left (signposted Beinn Ghainche) and park on the verge of the road beyond. Walk on to the end of the road and go through the gate to Sandhill Farm. Immediately beyond a sign points left for the Berneray Circular Walk.

Go left, through a gate, and walk along the bottom of the field beyond. Level with a house to your left, a sign points right. Walk up to a gate in the top corner of the field, with a cemetery visible beyond.

Walk up the right-hand side of the cemetery and continue to the top of the hill – there is no path, just find a dry line. The view from the top is superb.

Return by the same route.

21 Loch Bhuirgh _____ B

A low level walk over the machair, past a tidal bay then along the coast and back through the dunes. Wonderful coastal scenery. Length: **3 miles/5km**; *Height Climbed:* negligible.

O.S. Sheet 18

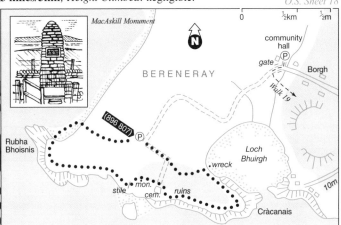

Follow the directions given for reaching Walk 19. Once you reach the hall at Borgh, however, go through the gate to the left (be careful to close it behind you) and follow the road over the machair to a small car park.

Park here and walk to the left, following a track through the cultivated ground. Leave the track when it turns hard right, heading half-right, up the slope, then descending to reach the shore of muddy Loch Buirgh near an old wreck.

Turn right along the shore of the loch and walk out to the rocky, grassy point of Cràcanais, then double back along the south shore of the island.

There is no path, but this is a pleasant walk over short-cropped grass; passing the ruins of black houses and then the island's cemetery. Beyond the cemetery, walk across to the obvious monument to Angus MacAskill – the 'Nova Scotia Giant'.

Looking ahead you will see a fence. Walk down to the end of the fence by the sea to find a stile. Cross this then continue behind the shore to the headland of Rubha Bhoisnis.

Walk north along the beach beyond for a short distance, then turn right, through the dunes (to avoid erosion, please use an existing path). Once through the dunes, the start of the walk will be visible ahead.

Valley is a tidal island off the north coast of North Uist, and you have a fair walk to get to it – it is 1¹/₄ miles/2km across the wet sand of the Valley strand. Length: **5 miles/8km** *(there and back); Height Climbed:* negligible. ***Tide tables will be necessary for this walk:*** *buy locally or consult http://easytide.ukho.gov.uk/EasyTide.*

O.S. Sheet 18

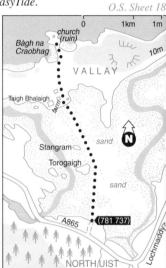

Check the tide tables before you go and aim to set off on a falling tide. Don't go in the mist – or if you do, take a map and compass and know how to use them. If you did get caught by the tide, you'd be unlikely to suffer more than wet trousers, but it could be cold and dismal.

Drive west from Lochmaddy (*Loch nam Madadh*) along the A865, round the north coast of the island, for about 12¹/₂ miles. The road takes a sharp turn right along the shore, at a junction with a minor road, and then runs past a plantation on the left. About halfway along the plantation, a rough track runs down to the shore. Drive down this track and park, being careful not to cause an obstruction. This is the main road to Vallay.

Walk down the track on to the strand. You can see Vallay ahead of you, and the small island of Torogaigh. Your way lies across the sand, going just to the right of Torogaigh, and right of the second, and smaller, island of Stangram.

Three ruins are visible on the island, with Taigh Bhalaigh (*Vallay House*) on the left, then a farm, then a cottage. Aim for the farm. Pass through a pair of gateposts on the shore then follow a grassy track to

the right of the farm and the farm buildings beyond. Follow the marshy track beyond, straight across the island and through the dunes to reach a secluded sandy bay: Bàgh nan Craobhag. Go round the bay and out to the point where you will find the scattered ruins of an old church: Teampull Orain. This is a fine place to watch the seabirds.

Return the same way. If you want to explore more of Vallay, remember the tide!

A walk round Lochmaddy on waymarked paths and public roads, with a short diversion to the mysterious Hut of Shadows. Length: **4 miles/ 6.5km**; Height Climbed: negligible.

O.S. Sheet 18

Hut of Shadows

From the pier in Lochmaddy, walk up past the Lochmaddy Hotel and turn right at a sign for the Uist Outdoor Centre. Go straight over the crossroads at the Sheriff Courthouse and continue to a T-junction, with the Outdoor Centre on the left. Go right here, past a house and along a track.

A sign for a public footpath leads you over a suspension bridge, with the imposing Sponish House (*Taigh Spònais*) ahead on the left. Beyond the bridge there is a junction. Keep right along a short wooden causeway and then on along the shore of Loch nam Madadh. The loch is filled with tiny islands and well-populated with seabirds and seals.

Close to the shore you will see a small, turf-roofed bothy. Duck through the narrow entrance into the pitch darkness. You're inside a camera obscura, a giant pinhole camera, and as your eyes become accustomed to the dark you'll see a picture of Loch nam Madadh projected on the wall. This is a live, moving picture, so watch for a passing fishing boat.

Continue round the shore to the join a track, then single-track road, which heads west, with the sea on your right and Loch Houram on your left. After about 1 1/2 miles/2.5km, turn left on the main road and follow it back to Lochmaddy.

On the flanks of Beinn Langais there is a magnificent chambered cairn, Barpa Langais, and one of the best stone circles in the Western Isles. This short walk takes in both these ancient sites, which date back 5-6000 years. Length: **2 miles/3km***; Height Climbed:* **250ft/80m**.

O.S. Sheet 18

Barpa Langais

Drive south from Lochmaddy (*Loch nam Madadh*) on the A867 for about 6 miles. Beinn Langais is the first hill that you see, on the left, and Barpa Langais is a prominent mound of white boulders on the slopes above the road. There is a sign on the main road for 'Barpa Langais', pointing left into a car park. If you come to the turn off for the Langass Lodge Hotel, you've gone too far.

From the car park (where there is some useful interpretive material) follow a clear path through a gate and up to the cairn. It was built before the peat started to form and must have been even more impressive when the ground level was 2 metres lower. Take a torch with you and creep

inside to see the massive pillars and roof slabs.

The path stops at the cairn but a string of waymarkers leads on beyond to the top of the hill. From the top there is a fine view over the watery landscape of North Uist, with the peaks of Burabhal (Walk 25) and Eabhal directly ahead. The waymarker posts lead you down the other side of the hill to the stone circle, built on a platform dug out of the hillside. Its Gaelic name is Pobull Fhinn ('Finn's People'), after the legendary Celtic hero.

From the stone circle, follow the path and then a boardwalk section to the Langass Lodge Hotel. Continue along the road back to the car park.

*This is a varied walk through a remote landscape with a steep ascent to the top of this appealing hill. Length **5 miles/8km** (there and back); Height Climbed: **400ft/120m**. If you're an experienced mountaineer, you might like to carry on and ascend Eaval (Eabhal). This would add an arduous 5 miles/8km, 1200ft/350m to your day.* O.S. Sheets 18 & 22

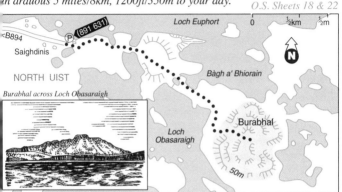

Unfortunately, this walk is right on the boundary of two OS maps, but the sea on one side and the lochs on the other should keep you on track.

From the junction between the A865 and the A867 at Clachan na Luib, in the south of North Uist, head along the A867 Lochmaddy (*Loch nam Madadh*) road for about 500m and turn right onto the B894 at the sign for Loch Euphort. Continue to the end of the road and park in the parking space.

Take the track that goes to the right of the house. Beyond the house, there is no obvious track, but go straight ahead through an open gateway. Follow a faint path over a low rise and down to an inlet, then continue along the shore with the sea on your left. Cross a narrow causeway over an outflow from the loch.

Follow the faint path. If you lose it, just keep heading for the obvious mound of Burabhal. You are between the sea and a loch and you can't wander too far off course. The path goes by a large boulder, with a silhouette similar to that of Burabhal, and then goes along the shore of the loch and crosses a fence at a cutaway section.

You are now below the hill, with a choice of ascents. You can go up either end, or up a broad gully opposite an island in the loch. The final ascent can be rocky. Return the same way.

This is only a short walk, but go at low tide and you will see seals. If you want a longer walk, the single-track road to the island is quiet and pleasant. This would add 3 miles/5km to the walk. Length: **1¹/₄ miles/ 2km** (there and back); Height Climbed: negligible.

O.S. Sheet 22

'Seal News'

Flodaigh is on the north coast of Benbecula (*Beinn na Faoghla*). Head north on the A865, and turn right just past the telephone box in Gramasdail, about 500m before the causeway to North Uist starts. If you want to walk along the road, park somewhere here.

Continue along the single-track road between lochans. Watch out for water lilies, seabirds and a ruined croft house standing on a small island. After crossing a short causeway, the road ends in a parking place. You are asked not to park here from 0800-0845 and from 1530-1630, when it is used by the local bus.

From the car park, take the right-hand track, which leads up a short rise to a gate. Continue along the track, through a second gate and then head downhill towards a house. After about 100m there is an abandoned car on the left. A copy of the Flodaigh 'Seal News' is usually taped inside the window.

As you follow the track towards the house, watch for a triangular boulder. Close by is a sign, on the ground, for 'Seal Point'. Leave the track here, following a faint path on the right to a gate in the fence. The path curves left to avoid boggy ground, then goes through a gap and leads down to the point. Approach quietly and enjoy the seals.

Return the same way.

This is the only high viewpoint on Benbecula (Beinn na Faoghla), which explains why Bonnie Prince Charlie spent several days and nights hiding here before his famous voyage 'over the sea to Skye' with Flora MacDonald. Length: **4 miles/6.5km** *(there and back); Height Climbed:* **330ft/100m**. *Possible extension to Ròisinis for experienced walkers with map and compass; this would add up to 6 miles/10km to the walk.*

O.S. Sheet 22

Ruabhal is an obvious landmark to the east of the A865. About 4 miles north of the southern causeway, or 2 miles south of the northern causeway, there is a sign for the 'Rueval footpath'. Drive down here and park by – rather surprisingly – a landfill site. Don't let this put you off, because you quickly leave it behind as you head out along the track. There's a wild and watery landscape ahead, and the heather slopes of Ruabhal above.

When the track runs along the shore of Loch Bà Una watch for a rough track heading up to the left, just before a small quarry. This track, and the faint path beyond, leads to the top of the hill. From here, there are great views north and south along the islands.

Return to the track. If you turn left it is possible to walk all the way to Ròisinis, from where Bonnie Prince Charlie and Flora MacDonald set sail.

28 Loch Druidibeag _____ B

This is a nature reserve – a wetland reserve, so be prepared for wet feet. Length: **4 miles/6km**; *Height Climbed: negligible. There is a possible extended circuit which takes you out on to the machair and around Loch Groigearraidh. The total length for this walk is* **5 miles/8km**.

O.S. Sheet 22

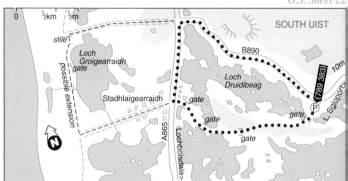

Head north from Lochboisdale (*Loch Baghasdail*) on the main A865 for about 15 miles. Turn right at a sign for Loch Sgioport (B890) and continue for about 1½ miles to a car park and information board.

Walk along a grassy track to two gates. Take the right-hand gate and follow a rough path through old peat cuttings. It can be marshy here, although planks have been laid across some of the worst sections.

Go through a second gate and down a narrow neck of land between the lochs. Go through a third gate here. Beyond the neck of land the path becomes faint. Bear right towards a white house. Beside this you will find a gate onto a track which leads onto the main road. Turn

right here and, after ½ mile/1km, turn right down the Loch Sgioport road back to the car park.

If you want to make the longer circuit, cross the main road and go down the narrow road on the other side. It is surfaced at first, and then becomes a good track across the machair. After about ⅔ mile/1km turn right along a track that runs through a gate and round the end of Loch Groigearraidh.

Cross the outflow from the loch on a footbridge. Go through a gate into a field and go right, along the edge of the field (by the loch at first). In the far right corner a stile leads onto a track. Turn right along this and it will lead you back to the main road and the start of the Loch Sgioport road.

This is a beautiful coastal walk along a fine beach. You can trim the length to suit yourself, but the distance given is for a circuit past Caisteal Ormacleit. Length: **5 miles/9km***; Height Climbed:* negligible.

O.S. Sheet 22

Turn off the main A865 about 8 miles north of Lochboisdale (*Loch Baghasdail*) at the sign for Bornais. Follow this road for just under a mile until it turns hard right. At this point turn left at a junction. Park close to the church at the end of the road.

Continue walking along the good track to reach Rubha Aird a' Mhuile – a rocky promontory with a small lochan, teeming with birdlife.

Go round the shingle dam at the end of the lochan and continue round the headland to reach the end of the long beach to the north. Here you have a choice. It is possible to walk along the beach, but there is no clear path through the dunes further north so it is difficult to know when to turn east. To follow the walk, it is easier to take the grassy track behind the dunes, with the fields to your right. The ruin of Caisteal Ormacleit will come into view ahead. Continue until you draw level with a fence crossing the machair towards the castle.

Walk up the left-hand side of this fence to reach a gate leading on to a track. A diversion to the left will lead to the ruined castle (built around 1700, for MacDonald of Clanranald, and burnt down in 1715 – do not enter, as the structure is unsafe). Otherwise, turn right to return to the start.

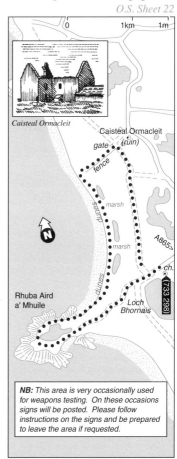

Caisteal Ormacleit

NB: *This area is very occasionally used for weapons testing. On these occasions signs will be posted. Please follow instructions on the signs and be prepared to leave the area if requested.*

This is one for archaeologists, but also for people who like flower-covered machair, silver beaches and Atlantic surf. Length: **2¹/₂ miles/ 4km**; *Height Climbed:* negligible.

O.S. Sheet 3

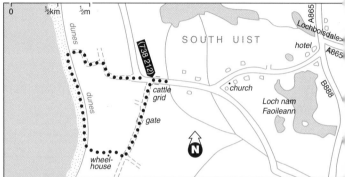

There is a wealth of archaeology hidden beneath the shifting sands of the Western Isles. The ruined wheelhouse on this walk is sometimes barely exposed, and it is easy to see how the sand could overwhelm the site again. The wheelhouse, or aisled house (a circular prehistoric dwelling with low stone walls and roof beams supported on a central post) has been tentatively dated to about 200AD.

Drive up the road from Lochboisdale (*Loch Baghasdail*) to the junction at Dalabrog. Turn left and then (immediately) right, in front of the Borrodale Hotel (*Cille Pheadair*). Continue past a church on the left, turn right at the T-junction and after about 500m park opposite some sheep pens.

Walk a few metres further along the road, across a cattle grid, then turn left along a sandy track across the machair. Ignore all turn-offs, and after about 500m, follow the track through a gate and continue with a fence to your left.

After another 500m you reach a four-way junction. Go right here, on a faint track leading in to the dunes. The track comes and goes, but if you follow the strongest line you should see the wheelhouse to your left after about 200 paces.

Keep straight on beyond to reach the beach. Turn right and head north. There is surf on the left and dunes on the right and a splendid solitude.

After about ¹/₂ mile/1km you come to the first obvious break in the dunes. Go through here and join a track running behind the dunes. Turn right along this and it will lead you back, across the machair, to the start.

1 Eriskay (*Eiriosgaigh*) _____ B

Eriskay is the island where Bonnie Prince Charlie first set foot on
Scottish soil and, more recently, where the SS Politician ran aground
with a cargo of whisky, inspiring the novel *Whisky Galore*. *This walk
goes along the Coilleag a' Phrionnsa, ('the Prince's Strand') and then
below Beinn Sciathan in the northern part of the island. Length:*
2½ miles/4km; *Height Climbed:* **330ft/100m.**

You can reach Eriskay by causeway
from South Uist or by ferry from
Barra. **From the causeway**, turn
right and follow the signs for 'Baile'.
From the ferry, drive to the north
end of the island, turn left at the T-
junction and follow the 'Baile' sign.

Continue along the road and park
near the Am Politicean bar. If you
go in here, you find information and
memorabilia about the shipwreck.

From the bar, walk along the road
past the graveyards. Keep right at the
fork. At a yellow waymarker, join a
grassy track that leads along the shore
and then go along the beach. This is
where Bonnie Prince Charlie landed,
and behind the dunes there is a
monument commemorating the event.

Approaching the end of the beach,
a track leads up through the dunes
to the road. Turn left, then almost
immediately right at a T-junction. In
200m a track starts to the left, through
a gate. Follow this uphill to a water
treatment plant.

At this point the track ends. Walk
straight up the hill behind the plant to
find a waymarker post. From now on
there is no path and you're following
posts: past the western end of Loch
Cracabhaig then left up a rocky gully.

O.S. Sheet 31

Watch for the wild Eriskay ponies.
(Experienced hill walkers might
attempt the short, steep climb of
Beinn Sciathan).

The waymarker posts lead you out
onto the road again, at the top of the
hill above the township. Turn right,
and when you pass the Community
Co-op bear left down St Michael's
Drive. A short path at the end of the
drive leads down to Am Politicean.

Ben Eòlaigearraidh is a straightforward ascent with spectacular views, and Tràigh Eais is a stunningly beautiful beach. Don't be tempted into the sea, the surf can be dangerous, but on a summer's day you can find warm pools on the beach deep enough for a swim. Length: **5 miles/ 8km***; Height Climbed:* **330ft/100m***.*

From Castlebay (*Bàgh a' Chaisteil*) drive north, around either side of the island. From the most north-easterly point on the road, turn off at the sign for Eòlaigearraidh and the airport. Park near the airport (famous for its beach runway).

Walk along the road, through the dunes and around the base of Beinn Eòlaigearraidh to the old church and graveyard of Cille-bharra (St Barr's Church). This is an early Christian site, with gravestones from Viking times (only a replica can now be seen) to the present day. The author Compton Mackenzie is buried here.

Continue along the road until it takes a sharp right turn at Bàgh nan Clach. A gate on the left leads on to marshy ground. The route is waymarked, but there is no path. The first waymarker is on the slope.

From this waymarker, head straight to the top of Beinn Sgùrabhal, where there are the remains of an Iron-Age fort. Descend to the east, to a second waymarker, then follow the waymarkers into a dip then up to the summit of Ben Eòlaigearraidh. Out to the east, you can see the cluster of small islands and Eriskay beyond (*see* Walk 31).

From the summit, head south

O.S. Sheet 3

down the grassy slope to reach a gate behind the north end of Tràigh Eais. This is a spectacular beach, especially when the big Atlantic rollers are coming in. If you explore a little, you'll find a roomy cave that featured in the film of *Whisky Galore*.

Walk south along the beach. Turn left before the rocks at the end of the beach to join a path through the dunes leading back to the airport.

Heaval looks like a mini-Matterhorn, dominating Castlebay (Bàgh a' Chaisteil). It is also a fine viewpoint. On a clear day you can see right down the chain of islands to Mingulay. Length: **4 miles/6km** *(there and back from Castlebay); Height Climbed:* **1250ft/380m**.

O.S. Sheet 31

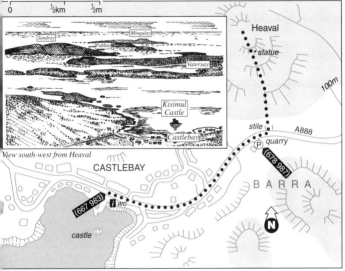

View south-west from Heaval

Heaval is not a big hill, but there's no path to the top and the summit is rocky. Be sure to take a map with you – if only to identify all the islands that you will be able to see.

There is a car park near the start of the climb: a mile east of Castlebay on the A888, just before a quarry. Alternatively, you can walk the first section, following the road from the centre of Castlebay. Either way, just beyond the car park, to the left of the road, there is a rickety stile leading on to the hill.

Follow the ridge to the summit. On your ascent, you will pass the statue of Our Lady of the Sea. Descend the same way.

If you want to make a day it, you can walk north along the line of tops that run up the centre of the island, descending at Loch an Dùin, close to the Northbay Hotel – over 5 miles/8km in total, one way, with steep undulations (map and compass needed).

A short loop through the beaches and grazing land of the southernmost inhabited island in the Western Isles. Paths rough; some waymarking.
Length: **4 miles/6km**; *Height Climbed:* undulating.

O.S. Sheet 3

Take the road signposted for Vatersay from the west end of Castlebay (*Bàgh a' Chaisteil*). Follow the road across the causeway and 2½ miles beyond to reach the community hall. Turn into a parking place 100m further along to the left. In the dunes on the right of the road you can see the memorial to the *Annie Jane* shipwreck.

Go through the gate, where there is a yellow waymarker post, and follow the path to the memorial and then on to the beautiful curve of Tràigh Siar. Turn left and walk to the south end of the beach, beyond which a waymarker leads over a stile. Follow the waymarkers around a cultivated area and up a low hill. At the top are the remains of Dun Bhatarsaigh, a 2000-year-old fort.

From the dun, the route is clearly waymarked, but there are no paths. Look for a waymarker to the south-east and descend to a stile. The next two waymarkers lead you across rocky and marshy ground to the grass-covered remains of an old wall. Follow this wall over a low hill to reach a transverse valley and the next waymarker.

Bear left here, down the valley, to reach the fence at the west end of Bàgh a' Deas (a short diversion straight on leads to a standing stone). Go round the end of the fence, taking care to avoid the deep cleft across on

NB: *A fence has been erected above the beach at Tràigh Siar. At time of writing (2009) there is no stile giving access to the beach. If this is still the case, turn left on the near side of the fence to reach the stile at the west end of the beach and follow the route from there (see map).*

the right, and on down to the beach.

The next waymarker is on the grassy promontory at the east end of the beach. Watch out for seals. The line of waymarkers now runs inland, across the short, dry turf of the machair, contours above the ruined settlement of Eòrasdail and then heads north below the rocky slopes of Am Meall.

The next waymarker is just over the skyline, above the sweep of Bàgh Bhatarsaigh. Follow the shore, then north along the beach. Rejoin the road at the far end of the beach.